T0149726

Within a Tear, a Smile and You

Ailsa Craig

BALBOA.
PRESS

A DIVISION OF HAY HOUSE

Balboa Press books may be ordered through booksellers or by contacting:

Balboa Press
A Division of Hay House
1663 Liberty Drive
Bloomington, IN 47403
www.balboapress.com.au
1 (877) 407-4847

Print information available on the last page.

ISBN: 978-1-5043-1223-3 (sc)
ISBN: 978-1-5043-1224-0 (e)

Balboa Press rev. date: 02/02/2018

Contents

Introduction

For you...

I can't see you
except within my dreams
I can't touch you
except within my thoughts
I can't feel you
except within my poetry
So, through the ink
of my pen
my words to you
will flow
until the ink runs dry
and trust, that
one day
my words
will find you.

- ailsa craig

Life presents us with so many varied moments, how we handle these moments is up to us and how they affect us. We all have to cope with loss and sadness, with pain and suffering, regret at missed opportunities; to what degree, depends upon our situation but we still have to find a path through it. On the other hand, happiness, joy, gain, love and nature, is felt the same in any situation and enjoyed and nurtured by those lucky enough to experience it.

Within my poetry, I try to paint a picture with words, I try to capture the essence of the moment, the feelings we express – desire, tears, beauty, strength, loneliness, friendship. I try to take you on a journey through these experiences, through nature, through friendship and through love.

This is my second poetry book and I hope you can feel what I am trying to express within the poems and prose; within my own experiences and those who have shared their lives and their stories with me.

Thank you for opening my book, please enjoy the journey,
With love,
Ailsa xx

Dedication

Casey, James and Callum
The light
in my life.
The smile
in my thoughts.
The laughter
in my belly.
The kindness
in what I hear.
The warmth
in what I feel.
The love
in my heart.
The hands
that never let go.
The gift
I have been given.
Thank you.
I Love you.

- Mumma

You are all I see and feel

When a gentle breeze
blows,
I feel your breath
through my hair.
When I see flowers
blooming,
I see the beauty in
your smile.
When I see the colours
of the ocean,
I see your eyes and the depth
of your soul.
When I marvel at the colours
of nature,
I marvel at your character
and the moods
you portray.
When I taste the fruits
of the earth,
I feel your soft tender lips
caressing me all over
as I ingest your flavours.
When I look to the moon
and the stars,
I am filled with love.
Their light guided me
to you.

To watch the brumbies run...

I sat up on the mountain
and watched the brumbies run.
They galloped along the valley
before the rains begun.
They came in many colours,
their manes so wild and long.
Their freedom was intoxicating,
this place was magic, like listening
to a favourite song.
I just waited until they
disappeared,
into the bush nearby.
What a sight to witness,
all I could do was sigh.
There are still these places
we can go to
and get lost in for a while.
Where man hasn't brandished
his demolition ball,
a place that fills your heart
and warms your smile.

The stars above.

The moment the stars
come out at night
and darkness draws the curtain
on the day,
I look into the blackness
of space
and wonder where you roam
or choose to stay.
I see the stars light up
so bright
as the moon peaks out from
the clouds,
I don't know where to turn
sometimes,
whether to remain silent or
shout out loud.
I sit in the silence
the darkness brings
and watch the bugs
dance in the light.
They are drawn to the brightness
of the lamp's yellow glow,
like us, follow the safety
of our sight.
I know that as I retreat
to my bed
and close my eyes and drift,
tomorrow will bring
a new day to think about
and through each thought
I will sift
and only keep the ones
that are real

and light up my day as well,
so that when the night
draws the curtain on the day,
I can sit in the darkness with
the stars above
and know my secrets to you,
I can tell…

If I close my eyes

As the sun sets
and darkness brings
the night,
I close my eyes
and find you
waiting
in my dreams…

When seabirds fly...

When the waves call
and the seabirds fly
and the froth of the sea
covers the sand.
When I hear my heart sing
to the sounds of the ocean
I feel part of this watery blue land.
When I see dolphins at play
and fish glide in schools
and the song of the whale is so clear.
When I feel the wind blow
and see cliffs stand on guard,
my senses are alive with no fear.
When I look to beyond
over the mass of blue ocean
I know there's a world down below.
When I feel with my heart
and fly with the gulls
I sink into the deepness I know.
When my boat crumbles and sinks
and sharks gather round
I keep my head up in order to live.
When I feel the sharp pull
and sense there's no hope
I know there's no more I can give.
But when the waves call
and the seabirds fly
and seashells adorn the white sand.
When I hear my heart sing
to the sounds of the deep
I feel safe when you reach out your hand.
When I walk with you
along picturesque shores

Ailsa Craig

and share this beautiful view.
I think of the times
I have roamed this beach,
it's a dream to be sharing it
with you...

Our footprints

Footprints of the past
may not seem to last
as the tides of time
remove them.
But only the outline
is taken away,
the person who walked there
will forever stay.
Etched in time
but vanished from sight.
The footprints one leaves
can be a blessing or
a blight…

My father's job...

It was a long drive
to the house on Banchory Station,
after we turned off the main road.
Our tyres churned up
the sandy earth
that covered the car
in a thick film of red dust;
so rich in orangey/red hues.
The cattle nearby
formed a line and peered at us
as we drove by.
An occasional guttural moo sound
was made
as they foraged through the
dry grassy land for something
to munch on.
The distinctive call of the crows
could be heard
as they perched in nearby gums.
It was dry and hot,
the sky was so blue and cloudless.
Banchory Station house,
surrounded by a huge veranda,
providing necessary shade from the heat of the sun,
stood majestically on the horizon
awaiting our arrival.
A red cattle dog
scampered up to us,
tail wagging and tongue out.
We were here,
the greeting was memorable.
The rest of our time
was a delight;

to ride with the stockmen,
to enjoy a billy tea around the campfire,
to hear stories city folk could not
imagine experiencing
and to enjoy the middle of nowhere.
As a fifteen year old,
it was a chapter from my story book.
Outback Australia,
I loved my father's job.

The tides of our emotions

Beautiful silence
as we sit
in the light of the moon
knowing confusion
is just a puff of wind
away.
Our boat sways gently
as the tide is drawn from the shore
and with it
my thoughts are pulled
away to a far distant
place.

I try not to let them
escape
as I use your strength
to attach them to.
Our boat is steady
in the moment,
securely fastened by
a connection,
in a tide,
that could go
either way.

Your path

Follow the path
you see in your dreams.
Let intrigue guide you
into the mystery
of what lies beyond.

The Cliff Top

On top of the cliff
I stand
looking out over
the ocean.
The waves are full of life
and pound
against the rocks below.
The spray reaches way
above
and sprinkles me with
a taste of the sea.
The wind is cool
as it tries to knock
me off my feet.
I wrap my jacket
around me tightly,
to keep the cold out.
It's beautiful, fresh and wild
but there's a whisper
in the wind.

Come with me
far across the sea
Where we can be
just you and me
Where you will find
within my arms,
love and shelter
from many of life's harms.

The words swirl around me
My thoughts dive into
the depths below.

Ailsa Craig

The fear it brings is softened
by the gentle hand
of the currents
as they guide my mind
to another world
across the oceans
into your gentle arms
and the warmth of your heart.

My new day...

I knew the day would come
when the line between
earth and sky
would merge
as it tried to configure
a new beginning.
I felt myself melt
into the colours of dawn.
Soft pinks and yellows
graced my palette
as I jumped from cloud to cloud
and left a smudge of colour
on each puff of white.
I skipped along
the sunbeams
that stretched into the sky
and was ablaze with
golden hues
an intensity I had never
touched before.
I floated on the calm
of the sea
as it carried me to shore.
It was a new dawn.
A new beginning.
The day was born
and I was ready
to embrace
my new life.

The connection...

To hear a distant call
you are in tune
with whoever
speaks to your
heart.

To feel a distant emotion
your heart is in sync
with whoever's
beat
is in tune with yours.

The key

When I am with you
it opens up a part
of my heart
that has been locked
by hurt.
Your smile seems to hold
the key.

Travelling days...

Take me back to places
where adventures fill
my heart.
With trails that go on
forever
and many friendships
we will start.
Where every morning
when you wake
and look out
to the way beyond,
your life is filled
with wonder
what the day will bring and
memories, of which
I'm fond.
So take me back
to somewhere
that makes me want to
write,
to express in words my feelings
of the people and wonders that
fill my sight.

After the seasons

As autumn leaves
fall on my heart
Winter closes in
and keeps us apart
When spring rains fall
and cleanse my way
I look forward to seeing
you again,
one warm summer day

His confusing love

Sunsets and broken fences,
clouds that cover blue,
flowers that smile
when you look at them,
reminds her of time spent with you.
Sand that's hot to walk on,
shells that cut your foot,
never knowing how you will react,
is like a fire place that covers you in soot.
Sunlight on the water,
raindrops falling from the sky,
cushions so fluffy and comfortable,
you know how to make her cry.
The moods of the day are changing
as each season brings its flavour to the mix,
you are complex, 'loving' and angry,
she wonders if it's too hard to fix.

The old lady's tear

The old lady
sits in her usual spot on the veranda
overlooking the bay.
The white wooden chair
has held her tiny frame for many years.
Her grey hair
falls loosely around her aged face.
A tear
rolls slowly over her cheekbone
as her watery eyes look
to the horizon.
She looks
for the life that eluded her,
looks for the love
she never found.
Her life
was nearing its end,
yet for others
it was just the beginning.
How she wished
it was her beginning.
How she wished
she could do it all again.
How she had learnt
just how quickly time passes.
How she had compromised
just to keep others happy.
Many scoffed
at her sorrow
and wondered at her sadness.
Had she not had
a good life
full of family and friends.

The one thing
that was missing,
that had only touched her life
just the once,
was far away from her now.
Her eyes still searched
into the way beyond
as her tears still filled
her heart
and the dream
she had hoped for
was just that, a dream.
As she waits for her end
and the sun to set
finally on her life.

Gentle touch

A gentle touch
upon my skin
is soft like velvet
and so warm with love.
A hug
from little arms
that goes on forever
and reached a place in me
reserved for those
who feel as I do.
Is it possible
that one's heart
can never be full.
Is it capable of
continuing to expand.
To house all those
who share your light,
your smile, your love
and yet there's
always room for more.
The little voice
that whispers in your ear
and soft ruby lips
that press gently against
your cheek.
Can time stop
for a moment
to cherish these touches,
these hugs,
these words.
I know one day
it will be no more.
I'll be a distant light

on a foreign shore.
A memory, that has long
since gone
but that gentle touch will
never leave my memory
and all the love
will keep my light glowing
should they ever need it
to guide their journey
home...

Study time

Darkness has fallen,
another day done.
Thoughts, words, smiles,
all go down with the sun.
The mind starts to wander,
have I done all that I should?
Maybe I can study some more,
if only I could
just finish this lot
and hand it all in
or screw it all up
and throw it in the bin.
Hmm maybe a glass
of vodka and lime,
yes, there's still a few hours,
plenty of time.
I'll do it tomorrow,
I'll get it all done
This time I'll finish
what I've begun
There's only two months
'til I qualify at last
More hours of typing
I'll be so happy to pass
and then I'll be someone
to help, guide and cure,
am I capable of doing this
or is it all too obscure
Maybe I'll just travel
and go back to Nepal,
go climb a mountain,
oh, such views to enthral
No, I'll do that the next day

after I finish this page,
it's taking me forever
and making me age.
Put down the pen
and just look at the moon,
tomorrow you'll finish
it'll be daylight again soon.

Within the...

Within the breeze
your thoughts are
carried
and gently placed
in my heart...

Within the sunlight
I feel your tender
touch
as I am immersed in
the warmth of the sun...

Within the rain
your tears do
flow
and wash away
my fears...

Within the moonlight
I sense your guidance
as I am led
out of darkness
into tomorrow...

Within the stars
is the magic
of a wish
as its sparkle
lights up
the evening sky...

Within a flower
is the scent of a woman
and her beauty
for all to
admire...

Within a rainbow
we find ourselves;
all the colours
that make up
a
beautiful arc
of light
of hope
of peace
of us...

Within a storm
our emotions
do conflict
and send a message
that all
is not well...

Within the tress
we see the strength
of a man
as each tree tries
to maintain its place
within the forest
but each vulnerable
to all
who yield the axe...

Within an adventure
new trails will
appear
leading you
to a back pack full of
memories...

Within a friend
is something special;
the beautiful gift
of friendship;
a connection
that you share and cherish
together...

Within nature
we are taught
a lesson in acceptance
our human class
is yet to understand...

Within a child
we find innocence,
love, trust, acceptance,
smiles, laughter and
imagination.
Then they meet
life...

Within the flame
lies the initial spark
that gave it life.
Be the spark
that lights up
the world...

Within your smile
you have the power
to make someone's day
very special…

Within my heart
I find you always.
Each time it beats
I am reminded
that we still have
time
to love…

When I'm gone

One day
I will no longer
leave footprints in your life.
One day
will be my last day
and that day
you will have no more
obligations to me.
No more need
to ignore me
and all that I do
and all that I am
will no longer
bother you
and you will
shine
in only your light.

To my son...

There's a smile in your voice
when you talk to me,
it makes me smile
like the sun has just come up.

You don't mind asking about my day
like it matters.
I'd rather hear about yours.

You listen to my tears
whether in laughter or in sadness;
your understanding
is beyond measure.

You have the ability to be positive
even if your day
may be the opposite.

You know my poetry
I can't get anything past you.

You make me realise
that there is still so much to learn
about others, about life.

You make me laugh
always,
sometimes until I nearly choke,
thank you.

How did I get so lucky?
You know me so well
and yet
I am still learning about you
as each new layer opens up
and exposes more vulnerabilities,
more compassion, more qualities
of you, my lovely son, my friend.

The message

If I toss a message in a bottle
far out to sea
will the currents
carry it
to its destination.

If I pluck a flower's petals
one by one
will the last one be
'He loves me'.

If I wish upon a star
will it light
a path
to my desires.

If I lie beneath the setting sun
will my heart
get burnt.

Or will my fears
be left behind
when the new dawn
rises
and a new beginning
picks me up
and I float away
on a whim
of a dream.

The beginning

When he asked me for
a dance
my head was filled
with romance.
He reached out
his hand
as we walked toward
the band.
He gathered me in
his arms
we flirted with all
our charms.
We moved to the rhythm
of the song,
it felt right that together
we belong.
The light was soft
and added to the mood.
Our hearts beat in
unison
as our attraction
ensued.
When the music
stopped playing
we still held each other
tight.
Was this the beginning
of a very special
night.

Into my imagination

As I wandered through the corridors
of my mind,
I came across a beautiful wooden door,
carved into the trunk of an old tree.
There was a sign etched into the wood –
'To my imagination'
No key was required
for I was the key
and it opened with a gentle nudge.
Before me lay nature
in all its beauty.
Green grass hills that rolled on forever,
snow-capped mountains with villages tucked in
high up on the peaks.
I see all the places I have visited, loved
and written poems about.
There are daisies everywhere I look.
I follow the flight of a seabird
as it takes me along the coast
to the ocean.
I could smell the familiar scent of the sea.
The water was green but blue and so clear
in its depths.
As the waves swam to shore,
they lay out an array of gifts on the sand.
Polished coloured stones and coral, beautifully
crafted shells; some of which got up and crawled
away via the crustacean living inside.
In the distance, I see a group walking towards me,
all laughing, dancing and waving as they approach.
Ah, it's you, all those who I love, who bring
meaning to my life, who make me smile.
Each one makes my heart sing.

Ailsa Craig

We sit together, they are all familiar now
to each other and share stories.
I look at them.
I look at the world that surrounds me,
the air is perfect as the colours of the sky tell me
the time is ending in my imagination.
I have to return to the corridors
of my mind
and revisit my reality.

Goodbye to you, my life...

As I journey
over my seas of tears,
I steer my boat
towards the mist ahead.
Within the mist
is a place
I've yet to discover;
a place in which
I'll find my memories
and faces
of times since passed.
I'll hold the hands
of those I once loved
and lost
and share conversations
of old.
As I look back
from whence I came
I see the faces and times
I now leave behind.
I feel such a strong pull
of emotions
as my connections are broken
and the sadness as each tie
frays
and eventually breaks.
It's such a deep despair
I feel
but I know there is
no return
as the winds of time
gently fill my sails

Ailsa Craig

and carry my boat towards
the end of my time;
the end of a life I was privileged
to live.

I opened the door

...and then I felt the breath of nature
...and then I heard the children's laughter
...and then I heard the song of the birds
...and then I heard the rustle of the leaves
...and then I felt the texture of the grass
...and then I could smell the perfume of the flowers
...and then I saw the colour of the sky
...and then I felt the sun caress me
...and then I felt the rain as it cleansed me
...and then I felt your lips so soft
...and then I felt alive

A moment in time

It's hard when the seas go calm
and there's no wave to carry you
or no wind to fill your sails
and take you away from
a moment in time.

It's hard when there's no more smile
and no arms to hold you
or no love to lift your mood
and take you into
a moment in time.

It's hard when the key is lost
and there's no replacement to open your heart
or no voice to beckon you beyond the door
that leads you
to a moment in time.

It's hard when the moment in time
is silenced
and all you've got
is a moment in time, in a place,
in a space,
where you don't belong.

When I was young...

When I was young
I could see beyond reality
I could dance in the clouds
and slide down a rainbow
I could climb to the top of the tallest tree
in the garden
and touch the planes as they flew overhead
I could skate across puddles frozen in winter
and dive into waves in the summer sun
I could make wishes on four leaf clovers
and dream of adventures in faraway lands
When I was young.

Yesterday's shadows

I see you
in the blue light
of the moon
as it lights up
the shadows of
yesterday's memories.

I feel you
in the yellow glow
of the sun;
your heart warmed my soul,
when yesterday was young.

I touch you
in the tears of the rain
as I remember the pain
of losing you
to yesterday's sorrows.

I hear your whispers
in the wind that blows
as it gently bestows
soothing words
from yesterday's voices.

I smile at you
in the faces I see
that ignite my memory
as yesterday smiles at me.

My bubble

Inside my bubble
I am floating
to and fro, around and around.
Floating through life
avoiding sharp points
of contact
ready to burst my surrounds
and send me flying
to earth
with a thud.
Inside my bubble
I see a contorted view
of my world
I see the colours of light
captured in a sunbeam;
passing through a prism and dispersing
into a rainbow.
If I float above the ocean
and catch a wave
I may drown
in my existing form
and become part of the watery film
that transforms me
and carries me to shore.
If I float above the earth
and let the vastness of the universe
carry me forever
through time and space;
escaping the pull of gravitation
I will wear the glow from the stars
that shine at night
and become part of the cosmic dust
as it captures my bubble

Ailsa Craig

and spreads my surrounds
into the way beyond
and there I will be released
and feel the beauty of
freedom and peace...

Look for me

One day
when the sky is blue
I hope I get the chance
to say 'hi' to you…

and even if
the rain does fall
I will always be ready
to heed your call…

So if you hear
the sound of a voice passing by
turn and look
and I'll try and catch your eye…

But if we miss
that moment in time
it will be hard to find
the right words
to finish my rhyme.

If I give you

If I give you my hand
where will you lead me.
Will we dance through the clouds
or sail across the sea.
Will we explore distant lands
and look for buried treasure,
or climb the highest mountain
and discover our true pleasure.
Will you sing me songs
and pull me in near.
Don't let me go,
don't leave me with a tear.

If I give you my smile
I will give you my hand.
Please hold it tight
as we venture to our new land.

If I give you my hand
I will give you my heart.
Always together.
Never apart.

Trapped

Street lights and broken signs
I see a shadow
lurking.
It stands so long
in the light that shines,
daunting in its presence.
I feel only fear.
A puff of smoke
from a cigarette
weaves its way through the glow.
Dark corners of the street
hide evil thoughts
ready to pounce
on unsuspecting passers-by.
I watch and turn
to walk away,
aware of the long shadow
that can capture me
in its presence.
The dampness of the night
hugs me
as I trip on broken pathways
and fall into
black holes of the past.
The long arms of the shadow
that lurks beneath the light
encase me
and take me back into
the shadows of yesterday.

It is within...

It is within the wild
I hear my heart beat
It is within the breeze
I hear voices from the past
It is within the oceans
I feel my blood flow
It is within the night skies
I see the stars in your eyes
It is within the rain
I feel the tears from your heart
It is within the mountains
I know my soul does roam
It is within the cry of the wolf
I feel your pain in my heart
It is within the sun
I can see my life unfold
It is within the darkness
I see my shadow wander
It is within the earth
I know I belong...

Empty feelings

We are together
We are alone
You are my life
But not my home

I see you coming
You watch me going
I feel the pain you give –
A gift unknowing?

You see me crumble
I see you smirk
You feel your power
But it doesn't work
(On me)

I look at you
You look at me
Your eyes are closed
To what they can't see

Until goodbye...

I can see
all that I can feel
I can feel
all that I can see

So take my hand
and hold it tight
Let me lead you
into the night

When dawn awakes
you'll feel me near
You'll know it's me
no need to fear

Your smile remains
even as you fade
Our life together
was heaven made

And when the time comes
for you to leave me
I know our light will shine
into eternity

I'm by your side
and I'll hold you tight
as life leads you
into the light

I can see
all that I can feel
I can feel
all that I can see.

Complicated...

Are you waiting by the tree
as I'm ready to leave
It's so complicated
if we fall.
Can we gather all our dreams
in a basket full of hope
and take them all with us
when we go.

Are you standing by the lake
where we sank in our boat
It's so complicated
we can't swim.
Can we gather all our pain
in a basket of despair
and throw it overboard
as we row.

Are you standing in the rain
where there's no place to shelter
Is it too late to see the truth
through the mist.
Can we bundle it all up
and toss it to the wind
and just be who we are
for awhile.

Or are the sins of our ghosts
still haunting our hearts
and taking the light from our lives
Is it too complicated
to take a leap of faith
and fly to the moon
one last time.

There is one, there is the other...

There are reasons, there are rhymes
There are moments, there are times.

There is loss, there is gain
There is love, there is pain.

There are smiles, there are tears
There is courage, there are fears.

There is peace, there is war
There is freedom, there is law.

There is you, there is me
There are the mountains, there is the sea.

There is cold, there is heat
There is win, there is defeat.

There is give, there is take
There is kindness, there is fake.

There is strong, there is weak
There is loud, there is meek.

There is illness, there is cure
There is wellness, there is pure.

There are the thinkers, there are the doers
There are the settled, there are the pursuers.

There are runners, there are walkers
There are shy ones, there are talkers.

There is colour, there is plain
There is sunshine, there is rain.

There are the tasters, there are the brewers
There are the ignorers, there are the wooers.

There is what you see, there is what you feel
There is what you dream, there is what is real.

There is straight, there is a bend
There is a beginning, there is an end.

Where there is one, there is another
One in the moment, one undercover.

There is calmness, there is strife
Toss the coin, this is life.

Sit still in peace...

Close your eyes
and imagine,
imagine a world
that is filled
with all your
dreams,
desires,
people you love.
Sit still and
stay there
awhile.
Immerse yourself
in these
thoughts.
How easy is it
to escape
into this world,
your world.
When you open
your eyes
you will feel
calmer,
better.
Maybe in time
you will find
that pathway,
that magic
that leads you
towards
your dreams
which then
become
your reality.

Ailsa Craig

WOMAD

Once a year
I'm so lucky
to hear
music from
around the world
and voices
I now recognise
as friends.

Abracadabra...

As far back as my memories go,
I remember sitting on the back step with whichever
furry friend graced our lives at the time.
I looked into the night sky and floated amongst
the thousands of stars twinkling around us.
I dreamt of adventures, happiness, friendship and love.
I have been given all these things in spade fulls
and the magic continues.
All these years later
I still sit and look to the stars
for answers, for magic.
Yet I know it's all around me
Abracadabra – it's life.

Dance of romance

Just a little dance
to put you in a trance
and take you to a place
within your own
romantic space.
When you dive into
his eyes
it will come as no
surprise
to find the music
that you share
makes you so much
more aware
of each other.

Just sit for a while...

Can we just sit
on a bench
and stare at the moon
and turn our silence
into a beautiful tune.

Can we just sit
on a bench
and feel so at ease
with just each other's company
enjoying the peace.

Our garden...

A flower
from your garden
you give to me.
A flower
from my heart
I give to thee.

A touch
from your finger tips
upon my skin.
I touch you with my eyes
showing you how
I feel within.

A kiss
laid gently
upon your lips.
A cup of emotion
from which your heart
sips.

A word
whispered
in my ear.
A word
I will remember.
A word I hold so dear.

Another dimension
is where we roam.
A place for our hearts,
our place, our home.

Tip toe...

Tip toe through the night time,
let the darkness hug your fears
and hide the shadows of the day.
Try to close your eyes
and see the colour in your dreams;
feel peace in your heart.
Let your mind rest
as the moon follows its passage
across the night sky
and let silence be the only noise
you hear as you sleep.
Do not worry about the next day
it will come and go
and give and take
whatever is to come your way.
Your day is filled with noise,
sounds, thoughts, voices,
all of which you react to
in appropriate ways,
affecting you in a good way
or a bad way.
The sun closes the day.
The sounds fade,
the mind plays with the day's thoughts;
they wrestle with your slumber
as darkness tries to caress you,
relax you and gently take your mind
to a place of rest and peace.
Until the sun awakens you
and leads you into another day,
tiptoe through the night time...

The cove...

Like the softness
of a flower's delicate petal,
your lips caress me.
Our senses
are taken to heights
of sheer rapture
then evaporate
in a cloud of golden sparkles,
showering us
in a feeling
of extreme oneness.
The waves
gather us in their arms
and carry us gently
along our passage
across the seas of our emotions.
The currents
steer us to a beautiful cove
where we are laid
together
upon soft white sand
adorned with jewels the sea
has gathered
on its journeys.
We have found our sanctuary,
a place where only we,
can be,
as one,
in divine peace.

Creag Ealasaid

(ailsa craig)

As we follow the bend of the road
down through South Aryshire,
we are greeted by the vast
Atlantic Ocean.
The fields are green,
the sky is grey.
The little burgh of Girvan
nestles around the bay before us
and there she is
looming on the misty horizon –
Ailsa Craig (Fairy Rock) –
my name's sake.
I have always felt drawn to her,
always,
as if I belonged to her.
My heart skipped a beat
I am finally here with you,
sharing you, this moment, with my family.
The seas are rough,
the winds are bitter
as we huddle with her for a photograph.
To share this moment
with the ones I love, is memorable.
Ailsa Craig is in my heart,
her wildness,
her steadfastness and strength,
her aloneness.
She is a safe sanctuary
for gannets and puffins
and those that needed shelter
in times gone by.

Ailsa Craig

As I stand before her
I feel like I stand before my judge.
Am I good enough
to bear her name,
to be her island
on the other side of the world.
Her ominous presence
intimidates me
but I feel protected,
she gives me strength.
She is wild, rugged and foreboding
in the stormy seas that surround her
but when all is calm
she is a presence, an identity
that takes on any mood
she finds herself in.
My soul is home.

Into the light.

I see the light
it comes to me
and takes me to
infinity.
I see beyond
day and night
I feel only love
within this light.

A new page...

As she looked down
to the blank page
before her,
a single tear fell
from her eye
and spread from
corner to corner
on the empty sheet;
like a drop of ink on
blotting paper.
In its wake,
words appeared
one by one
until they formed
a message.
She felt the pain
in her heart
subside
as the tear's inscription
spoke to her.
"It's time, turn the page.
New words are waiting
to be written.
Let the ink flow
and allow yourself
to feel again."
As she looked up,
she smiled,
grasped her pen
and turned the page.

Today Tomorrow Forever

She walked a path that led to 'somewhere'
using signs to show her the way.
Sometimes confused by experiences she stepped into
or by personal happiness that didn't want to let go.
But still she wandered,
sometimes tempted
by the green grass on the other side of the path,
trying to lure her with false signs.
Sometimes finding herself in a maze of pathways
when the signs were difficult to recognise.
And on she wandered,
not knowing what lay before her
but knowing she wasn't there yet.
The path took her across oceans of water
to faraway lands, over mountains and rivers,
along sandy shores and through forests of trees.
Each time she thought she was there
another sign would light up and on she would go.
She grew tired at times; her mind grew weary.
The signs would say 'rest here for a while'
and when she was refreshed and renewed, on she would wander.
One day, while on her journey, she saw a light up ahead,
it just felt right to stop here.
As she bathed in the light,
a hand reached out and gently clasped hers.
An immediate sense of calm came over her.
"Am I here?", she wondered.
Another sign appeared through the light –
'Today, Tomorrow, Forever'
The path still lay before her, but now she shared it
with another.
Now it all made beautiful sense and on they strode,
together, forever.

Silent words...

Often silence
speaks with the loudest
voice.
When spoken
intentionally,
can be more hurtful
than audible words.

Ailsa Craig

Always with me...

You walk with me
in my everyday shadows,
always there
when
I walk in the light.

Remembrance Day - (To dear Dad)

I hear the winds are calling
all my mates from long ago;
all my companions who I fought with
and stood together, toe to toe.

We are meeting at the mess hut,
we're all up here 'cept a few.
Jock and Robbie are laughing,
still the jokers of our crew.

We flew many a mission
and faced many bombs and flack.
I was so glad to be your pilot
and make sure we all got back.

So raise your glasses lads,
to our mates who we do love.
We've been to visit hell and back,
now we're together up above.

A moment of care...

There comes a time,
a moment, a space,
which appears to mirror
confusion on our face.
It's filled with emotion,
filled with wonder,
sometimes anger, sometimes grace.
We look away,
but the barrier is still there;
the moment in time
in which we care.
What to do
and what to think.
Just stop now,
it's time to blink.

The sunset of a life...

Some days come
and bring some news,
sad for you to hear.
It makes you look at life,
dear friends and family and
all that you do fear.
When a family member
is taken
and there's nothing you
can do,
to help those most affected
with loss and a broken heart too.
You can wrap your arms
around them
and send notes
of sympathy and love,
but the loss is felt so deeply
as a new light drifts
into their sunset up above.

Your call...

I hear your call
in a distant voice
overseas seas filled with waves
and mountains covered in snow.

I hear your voice
in the sounds that surround me;
in the song of the bird
and the wind through the leaves.

I hear your laughter
in the happy times I spend with friends;
in the moments we enjoy
and faces filled with smiles.

I hear your sadness
when I am alone
or feel fear walking empty
pathways
where no friends are found.

I hear your cries
in the pain suffered by
those close to me
and I can't mend their broken
hearts.

I hear your call
in the voice of the wild.
It beckons me to come
with a voice that gets louder
at the fold of each day.

A tear drop on my pillow...

There's a tear drop
on my pillow
for all the light
that has left my life.
All the beautiful souls
that once touched
my heart.
As I look out into the nothingness
that surrounds me,
I know it is filled
with memories, with love,
the distant sounds of laughter,
and music shared.
You walk on a different path now;
you are a new sparkle in an ever
growing sphere of light
that one day will welcome
all of us, one by one,
and into the glow, we will merge
and be home.

Walk with me...

Walk with me,
hold my hand.
Share my smile
and feel what I feel.

Walk with me
and feel my heart.
Share the beat
and we'll walk in time.

Walk with me
and fill this moment.
Share this time
with what we are.

Walk with me
through this dream.
Share the colours
we do paint.

Walk with me,
let our light guide us,
through the darkness
into tomorrow.

Just walk with me...

Life's dance...

We all dance to a different tune,
orchestrated in various ways.
Some tunes enchant us;
stimulate needs and desires
within us
and sweep us away
like a beautiful ballet
that brings tears to our eyes.
Other tunes lure us in,
like a siren's call;
enticing us into dangerous waters
that drown our hearts
and hypnotise our emotions,
or causing us to lose our balance.
We dance, we tiptoe, we waltz
through life's musical production,
sometimes adding extra notes to our tunes,
to enhance the vibrancy
and quicken our step.
Each ensemble as interesting as the next,
until,
the last sheet of music is turned,
the conductor's baton is laid to rest and
the orchestra becomes silent.

For you...

I can see the sunshine playing
with your hair
I can see the blue sky
in your eyes
I can see our laughter
in your soul
I can feel the sunshine
in your arms
Can you hear the music
that we play?

With you,
is like being in an endless
summer day...

The train ride...

The train rattled on
as I stared out into a world
racing by.
Houses, trees, lives.
all passing by in a moment
so fast.
Stories unfolding,
conversations ensuing,
coffee beans brewing,
laughter being shared.
Tears being shed,
love's initial bloom,
babies being born
and last breaths exhaling.
My thoughts were flying
through me
as rapidly as life was passing me by,
outside the window on the train.

You...

The door opened easily,
I thought I would need a key.
As I wandered into the room,
the door slowly closed behind me.
There was music playing
I recogised the song,
one which brought tears
to my eyes,
I hadn't heard it for so long.
A voice strong but gentle
called out my name.
I looked to where it was
coming from
and noticed a window pane.
I opened up the window,
the air was fresh and warm.
I saw a figure standing there;
just standing on the lawn.
He turned ever so slowly
as I looked to see who it was.
My heart started beating
so rapidly.
I couldn't believe my eyes
because –
it was you.
At last,
it's you.

The woods of doubt...

A walk in the woods
can be daunting
when you let memories
haunt you.
Confrontation with fear
can bind you to your past
and make you miss
a path laid out for 'you'.
An opportunity placed
in your hand
is lost
when you trip over the hurdles
you placed on your path.
The woods you find
yourself in
can get crowded with pathways
should you choose your fear
over trust.
Which path to take?
Which one did I miss?
As you wave goodbye
to a dream
you thought
was never possible.

'Somewhere'

The seas were calm with a slight rise
in the waves that lapped the shoreline.
The mountains that loomed above,
imbued in a dark green haze,
were covered in a cloud of mist.
Our small boat,
creaked its way towards the rocky outcrop
guarding the shore.
What is this place
to which we have been guided?
An eerie silence greeted us,
bar the odd squawk of the seabirds,
circling way above the strangers
about to set foot on their domain.
We grabbed what we little we had
and scrambled over the array of
sharpened rocks and crustaceans;
careful not to cut our already
sea damaged feet,
which sank with delight,
into the course, damp sand
that awaited us behind
the rocky obstacle course.
It felt good to walk again;
to stand upright
after weeks of sitting in our
little wooden boat.
'We are here, 'somewhere'.
'Somewhere' is a place;
it is our place,
until such time we are asked to leave.
In front of us lays a sea of green foliage.
In here, we will find,

materials for our shelter,
materials for our comfort.
materials for our survival.
Until we are missed,
we will not be found.
'We will 'be',
what this 'somewhere'
allows us 'to be'.

My spirit love...

Red and gold
Green and blue
Silver sparkles
and I'm thinking of you.
Decorations
for Christmas cheer,
presents wrapped,
I feel you near.
All this time
I thought you'd gone,
either to another world
or a new love has been born.
But here you are
so vivid in my mind,
thanks for visiting me,
your soul is so kind.
I won't forget you,
even though time can cause a rift.
I won't forget you,
you were such a special gift.
The Christmas tree shines
with love and good cheer,
you are my soul spirit;
so far in body, but in my heart,
so near.

Shadowland

What if there is another dimension
We can see it
We see it everyday when we stand in the light
Another world
that gives life to our shadows
A peaceful world
that can't be touched only distorted
by acts of nature – wind, rain, darkness and movement.
I guess in our world
our truths are distorted
not by nature
but by the nature of us
We can add colour to ourselves with make-up and clothes,
with words and descriptions.
But in Shadowland
we are completely ourselves
We can't touch that world
only see it for what it is
and when the light fades, we disappear
until such light
brings us to life again.
The same applies in our dimension –
when we stand in the light
others can see us, feel us, connect with us.
When we disappear into the shadows
the light can't reach us
and neither can those
who could perhaps
make our light sparkle brighter than we ever could
imagine…

Waves of emotion

The waves of my emotion
are hitting me fast.
The waves of my emotion
are sweeping right past.

So tell me, tell me
tell me who I am.
So tell me, tell me
tell me you are my man.

If only I could see you
then maybe I'd understand.
If only I could see you
instead of a wave from your hand.

So give me, give me
give me all you can.
So give me, give me
a road to another land.

It doesn't ever feel right
not having you around.
It doesn't ever feel right
I'm not steady on the ground.

So tell me, tell me
tell me who I am.
So tell me, tell me
tell me you are my man.

I wish that you could know me
and see me for who I am.
I wish that you could know me

then maybe we can make a plan.

So give me, give me
give me all you can.
So give me, give me
a road to another land.

The waves of your emotion
are as high as they can be
The waves of your emotion
are sweeping over me.

So tell me, tell me
tell me who I am
So tell me, tell me
tell me you are my man.

Hello...

That smile you give,
it gets me every time.
That look I see
I know it's only mine.
Every time I see you,
it's been in a different place.
We walk the same path,
though,
maybe at a different pace.
It's so nice
when you look my way.
It really helps to add
such a sparkle to my day.
I wonder what you think
when you turn
for a second glance.
I think we are both
so very shy,
we always miss our chance
to say
more than just
'hello'.

The mask...

She knew what
awaited her this day.

She knew
she had choices.

She could feel
her internal self, constrict.

She knew
she had to face her fear.

She found her mask
and fixed it into place.

She closed down
the person she really was.

She smiled, she dressed,
she was ready.

A tear fell.

Christmas wink...

The Christmas presents
were all under the tree.
The children's faces
were smiling with glee.
The tree was alight
with beams of gold;
magical in a child's eye
and even for the old.
We passed around the gifts
with love and a smile.
I haven't seen so much laughter
in such a long while.
With toys and chocolates,
books and games,
perfume and underpants,
socks with names.
Fancy food served,
oh, such a treat.
Nibbles and plum pudding,
so much to eat.
We sat together laughing
enjoying the day,
now time for a cricket match,
yes, time for a play.
The night time came
and we sat around with a drink,
as I looked at the Christmas tree
I'm sure it did blink.
'Merry Christmas'

Merry Christmas

Smiles and grins
Tonics and gins
Shortbread and prawns
Late nights and yawns
Giving is fun
Since time first begun
Seeing you happy
With the camera, I'm snappy
Family and friends
Broken heart mends
What Christmas does bring
Can certainly, make your heart sing.

If loneliness is present
Please look up above
Look to the stars
We send you our love.

Merry Christmas to all
Wherever you may be
You're all so very special
Always, to me…

Sigh...

Ah, I feel your soft, velvet touch
against my skin
as you gently encase me
into your aqueous world.
Your calmness
relaxes my senses
as I float like a cloud
amid your cool blue waters
away from all that I know
into the peaceful oblivion
of your ocean.

When...

When the sky is blue
what are you going to do
just contemplate your shoe
or show the world you.

When the sky is grey
do you feel a certain way
and just waste the hours away
or make the most of your day.

When it's dark at night
and you've turned off the light
do you switch off your mind
and peace do you find
in dreams you escape to
and live the real you.

When you wake in the morning
and realise after yawning
that the smile on your face
was found in a place
where a walk through a dream
could be more than it may seem.

If you decide to make it real
then go after what you feel
(whether skies are grey or blue)
is right for 'you'.

Life is light. . .

Through light we travel.
We shine then gradually fade
as the light within dims
and we merge into
the darkness of our sleep.
Our memory, our essence, remains
as our light is passed on through another and another.
The darkness can only swallow
that which serves us no more.
The body; the vessel that carried
our sparkle through life's glow,
withers with time
until it is no longer required
and the light stays dim
and waits, until
a new vessel is ready
and this light of life
can shine once more.

Wherever I go.

Wherever I go
I will take you with me.
Whatever mountain I climb
or rough seas I cross,
I will use your strength.
If I am cold in winter
or alone in an unfamiliar place,
I will use your sunny smile
to warm me
and the light in your heart
to guide me to a safe place;
for you are my life
and the reason I live.

My country, my home...

As I wander far and wide
and view the world
from the other side,
my heart is sad
for the Great Divide
and anything else
Australia can provide.
For it doesn't matter
who you are or how far you roam,
your heart will always yearn
for the place you call home.

Moonlight...

Oh moon,
shine thou light
and make a twinkling pathway
across the water
to our safe haven.

Thou light
is soft and clear
as it traverses
across the seas
through the darkness
of the night
that blankets our world
and hides dangers
and noises that
prickle down our spines.
But this light does gives us
calm and serenity
to take us into the
dawn of a new day.

Fields of past...

Walking through
a golden field of memories,
my fingers caress
the tops of the long yellow grasses.
I feel the dew drops
gently resting on the stems –
the tears I have shed
for all who have passed.
My field is growing
year by year.
The grass gently
sways in the breeze.
I feel a surge of sadness grip my heart,
but never want my field
to fade or cease.
As life goes on
I see distant smiles,
their warmth feeds the field
with memories of laughter
and times once shared.
It tells me
how quickly life goes by.
As my field grows
the memories become
a part of,
a place visited,
a time remembered,
a place to shed a tear,
a warm smile and a loving sigh.

Our time...

Remembering a time
we drank vodka and lime
when I was yours
and you were mine...

We did not speak –
Our hearts had
already made themselves
comfortable...

We did not need to touch –
Our eyes had
danced together
all night...

To see or not to see...

It's up to you
whether you use
your eyes
or
your heart

In my dreams...

When the sun goes down
and the moon lights a pathway
to our dreams,
I follow the glow to your world.
As I think of you
I see your face,
your eyes,
your smile,
but you are nowhere to be seen.
Only in my dreams
I feel your breath
so close.
Your arms are around me.
The heat of your body
warms me
in ways I have never known.
Your closeness invites my desires
but when I turn
you are no longer there.
You are far way;
far away in another world.
A world
I don't belong in.
So, I will have to make do
with the dark of the night
bringing you to me.
Bringing your breath,
your touch,
your eyes,
your kiss,

Ailsa Craig

when I shut my eyes
and
I find you waiting
in my dreams.

Until then...

Until the ocean
sends her last wave
to shore,
I will wait for you.

Until I no longer
feel your warmth
from the sun,
I will wait for you.

Until I no longer
see you in the smiles
that greet me each day,
I will wait for you.

Until I no longer
hear your song
in the bird's morning chorus,
I will wait for you.

Until the sun
takes her final bow
and darkness draws the curtains
on my life,
I will wait for you.